ALSO BY KURT ANDERSEN

Heyday

Turn of the Century

The Real Thing

RESET

RESET

HOW THIS CRISIS
CAN RESTORE OUR VALUES
AND RENEW AMERICA

Kurt Andersen

Foreword by Tom Brokaw

RANDOM HOUSE   NEW YORK

Published in the United States by Random House,
an imprint of The Random House Publishing Group,
a division of Random House, Inc., New York.

RANDOM HOUSE and colophon are registered trademarks of
Random House, Inc.

A portion of this work originally appeared, in different form,
in the April 6, 2009, issue of *Time* magazine as
"The End of Excess: Is This Crisis Good for America?"

Library of Congress Cataloging-in-Publication Data

Andersen, Kurt,
   Reset : how this crisis can restore our values and renew America /
by Kurt Andersen.
      p.   cm.
   ISBN 978-1-4000-6898-2
   eBook ISBN 978-1-58836-964-2
   1. Financial crises—Social aspects—United States.   2. United
States—Economic conditions—21st century.   3. United States—
Social conditions—21st century.   4. Values—United States.   I. Title.
   HC106.83.A53 2009
   303.3'720973—dc22

                                                    2009019711

Printed in the United States of America on acid-free paper

www.atrandom.com

2 4 6 8 9 7 5 3 1

First Edition

Book design by Liz Cosgrove

For my parents, Bob and Jean Andersen

Author's Note

Sincere thanks to Rick Stengel, who planted the seed that grew into this essay, an earlier and much shorter version of which he generously published in *Time*. (A few sections of the book appeared previously in *The New Yorker* and *New York*.)

Foreword

Tom Brokaw

A friend, a successful businessman with temperate consumption habits, suggests that America adopt a new mantra as it emerges from this hangover brought on by reckless excess. "We should get up every morning and ask, 'What do I need?' Not 'What do I want?' "

That strikes me as a simple but profound prescription to deal with the devastating effects of the binge that has defined so much of our recent past. It is also a useful code to follow as we design a more sensible future.

What has encouraged me greatly as I travel around the country, from the shaken baronies of Wall Street to the regional centers of commerce and back roads of rural America, is the common acknowledgment not just that a course correction is overdue, but that this is an exciting opportunity to construct a new model that will serve us better for the challenges ahead.

To do that will mean some serious attitude adjustment about how we calculate need versus want. Does everyone really qualify as a home buyer, or is it more realistic to admit that some are destined to rent? In this era of energy concerns, isn't it more sensible to build more efficient common-wall houses in larger green spaces than more McMansions on tiny lots?

In fact, housing, the temptress that caused so much of this trouble, is a metaphor for how we should emerge. The damage has been done. It is time to clear the wreckage and rebuild on a new foundation that can weather whatever storms come our way.

The new American economic culture should be about proportion and function, efficiency and accessibility.

In this provocative and insightful book, Kurt Andersen has given us a blueprint for what can be a new way of seeing America as a land of opportunity and sound values. How we respond to these challenges is a fundamental test of all of us.

RESET

ONE

We Let the Good Times Roll

Let's be honest: we all saw this coming for a long, long time.

In the early 1980s, right around when Ronald Reagan became president and Wall Street's great modern bull market began, we Americans gave ourselves over to gambling (and *winning*). We started thinking magically. From 1980 to 2007 the price of the average new American home quadrupled, and almost doubled even after adjusting for inflation. The Dow Jones Industrial Average climbed from 803 in the summer of 1982 to 14,165 in the fall of 2007—a 500 percent increase after inflation.

From the beginning of the 1980s through 2007, the share of disposable income that each household spent paying off its mortgage and consumer debt increased by 35 percent. Back in 1982, the average American household saved 11 percent of its disposable income, but then the percentage steadily dropped, to less than 1 percent in 2007.

Not coincidentally, it was during this same period that state-sanctioned and state-run gambling became ubiquitous in America. Until the late 1980s, only Nevada and New Jersey had casinos, but now twelve states do, and forty-eight of the fifty have some form of legalized betting. It's as if we decided that Mardi Gras and Christmas are so much fun we ought to make them year-round ways of life.

We started living large literally as well as figuratively. From the beginning to the end of the long boom, the size of the average new American house increased by half, even as the average family became smaller. During the two decades ending in 2007, the average new American car got 29 percent heavier, 89 percent more powerful, and 2 percent less efficient. Meanwhile, the average American gained about a pound a year, so that an adult of a given age is now at least twenty pounds heavier than someone of the same age during the 1970s. Back in the late 1970s, 15 percent of Americans were obese; more than a third of us are now.

We saw what was happening for years, for decades, but we ignored it or shrugged it off, not quite believing that push would really, finally come to shove. The U.S. automobile industry has been in deep trouble for decades. Detroit's unprofitability this last year has been breathtaking, but as long ago as 1980 (the year the federal government first bailed out Chrysler) newspapers were regularly carrying headlines about "record losses" at the car companies. Since 1983, GM's share of the American car market has steadily shrunk, from 43 percent to 22 percent. Yet all along, cheap oil and occasional upticks—minivans and pickup trucks and SUVs! Saturn! the PT Cruiser!—have prolonged the great denial, sustaining an increasingly desperate wishfulness that the good old days might somehow return.

For a decade now, ever since the Web really took off, almost every part of the old-media industry—newspapers, magazines, network TV, local TV, records, advertising—has been in trouble, with only the rate, speed, and severity of shrinkage in question. But until very recently, most of them were managed as though their businesses wouldn't, couldn't ever really, finally die. But newspapers' circulations are now evaporating at a stupendously accelerating rate—by 5 and 10 and 20 percent a year—and last year Americans bought fewer than half as many CDs as they did in 2000.

We watched the median household income steadily decline since the end of the twentieth century . . . but, but,

but our houses and our 401(k)s were ballooning in value, right? Even (and sometimes especially) smart, proudly rational people engaged in magical thinking, acting as if the miraculous power of the Internet and its "new economy" would somehow, miraculously, make everything copacetic again. We all clapped our hands and believed in fairies. We gorged on free lunches.

The popular culture tried to warn us. For twenty years now, we have had Homer Simpson's spot-on caricature of the quintessential American—childish, irresponsible, willfully oblivious, fat and happy. And more recently, there was *WALL·E*, with all of humanity reduced to Homerized refugees from a despoiled earth. There was also a profusion of darker speculations concerning our decline and fall—some fact based, some entirely fictional, but all expressions of a shared and growing sense that our recklessness and complacency were sending us over the falls. There were news stories warning of a real estate bubble back in 2005, years before the bubble burst. Every season saw some new comparison of the United States to the late Roman Empire by authors of every ideological stripe. There were also the Left Behind novels, Cormac McCarthy's *The Road*, end-of-the-world feature films (*The Day After Tomorrow, 28 Days, I Am Legend*) and documentaries

(*An Inconvenient Truth*), and a rise of hysterical chatter about the cosmic meltdown scheduled by the ancient Mayans for 2012.

Even in opinion polls taken last year, before the crash, between 70 and 85 percent of Americans were saying they thought the country was "on the wrong track." We knew, in our heart of hearts, that something had to give.

Especially those of us of a certain age. Remember when each decade, not long after it finished, assumed a distinct character? We all knew and know what "the '50s" mean, and they definitively ended with the Pill, JFK's assassination, and the Beatles. Then "the '60s" ended when countercultural utopians abandoned their fantasies and everyone else got tired of being perpetually alarmed and hectored. And "the '70s" ended when stimulants overtook depressants as America's substances of choice, and AIDS appeared.

Yet in all salient respects, "the '80s"—as defined by Reaganism's reshaping of the political economy, the enthralling introduction of PCs, and the vertiginous rise in the stock market—*simply never ended.*

It's as if the Roaring Twenties, instead of crashing to a halt in 1929, had lasted all the way until 1945, uninterrupted by a depression or world war. Despite the recession of

1990 . . . and the popped bubble in technology stocks in 2000 . . . and then another recession . . . and the terrorist attacks in 2001 . . . despite all of it, the 1980s spirit endured, like an awesome winning streak in Las Vegas or a multigenerational rave that went on and on and on. The Soviet Union collapsed: *yes!* American-style capitalism triumphed and spread: *hooray!* So what if every year since the turn of the twenty-first century the U.S. economy was growing much more slowly than the global economy? The (Chinese-made) stuff we were all buying at Walmart and Costco and H&M stayed supercheap—as did money itself, which our new best friends, the Chinese, obligingly supplied to us by the low-interest-rate trillion. The fresh technological miracles and wonders just kept on coming, reinforcing our sense that progress was on the march and magic was in the air. Even 9/11 and our resulting Iraqi debacle, after a while, came to seem like mere bumps in the road.

Deep down we had an inkling at least that the spiral of over-leverage and overspending and the prices of stocks and houses bubbling ever higher were unsustainable, just as everyone figured that the unprecedented performances of baseball players like Barry Bonds and Roger Clemens couldn't be kosher, but . . . no one wanted to be a buzz kill. From 1982 until 2008, we partied like it was 1999.

TWO

Life in the Casino Economy

My own aha (or uh-oh) moment occurred two and a half years ago. Out in Omaha, where I grew up, I happened to share a ride to the airport with a pair of United Airlines pilots. Both were classics of the type—trim, square-jawed, silver-haired, twangy-voiced white men, one wearing a leather jacket. Sam Shepard and Paul Newman could've played them in a movie. This was more than a year and a half before the economic emergency began, back when most of us were still feeling pretty swell about the financial end of things. The pilots spent the entire drive sputtering and whining—about being baited and switched when their employee ownership of the airline had been disintegrated by its bankruptcy, about the default of their pension plan, about their CEO's 40 percent pay raise, about their loss of trust in the company to which they'd devoted their whole careers, and, in effect, about turning from right-stuff demigods who worked hard and played by the rules into disrespected, sputtering, whining losers.

The next morning back in New York City, I read the news about record-setting bonuses on Wall Street, an aggregate amount 1,100 percent higher than in the super-go-go year of 1986. I calculated that the revenues at just one of those money-minting firms, Goldman Sachs, were larger than the GNPs of two-thirds of the countries on earth—a treasure chest from which Goldman was disbursing $53.4 million to its CEO and an average of $623,000 to everybody who worked at the place.

Ordinarily, I would have shrugged and moved on with New Yorkerly indifference—notwithstanding their reduced pensions, the pilots were still flying, and I wouldn't trade my life for any banker's. But I wasn't able to stop thinking about my jump-cut visions of those defeated pilots in Omaha and the mega-bonused Wall Street guys shopping for $15 million apartments. And as a result, that holiday fortnight felt to me fully Dickensian—the jolly, prosperous bourgeois bustle and glow, as usual, but also in the foreground the conceited, unattractive rich, our Dombeys and Bounderbys and unredeemed Scrooges.

Until that moment in 2007, I had repeatedly ragged on Lou Dobbs's nightly hour of angry populism on CNN. But then I suddenly, viscerally understood Dobbs's followers' rage and disgust about the ongoing breaches of the social contract, an American economic system that seemed more and more rigged in favor of the extremely fortunate. During the last quarter century, we had not only let economic uncertainty and unfairness grow to grotesque extremes but also inured ourselves to the spectacle. As America had become a lot more like Pottersville than Bedford Falls, people closer to the top of the heap simply shrugged and moved on.

At the bubble's maximum inflation point, the asymmetry between the Goldman boss's eight-figure compensation and that of his average employee—eighty-five times as large —was virtually socialistic by comparison to the ratio that prevailed in the rest of the economy. An average American CEO has been getting paid *several hundred* times the salary of his average worker, a gap an order of magnitude larger than it was in the 1970s. In Japan, the ratio is just eleven to one, and in Britain twenty-two to one. Back in 1980, the Chrysler CEO Lee Iacocca's salary was $868,000, which put him among the top one hundred highest-paid

American CEOs. That salary in inflation-adjusted dollars, around $2 million, wouldn't even get him a place in the top four hundred today.

This is not the America in which we grew up. Back in the 1920s, the richest one-half of 1 percent of Americans received as much as 15 percent of all income, but from the 1950s through the 1970s the income share of the superrich was cut back, reasonably, by more than half. The rich were still plenty rich, and American capitalism worked fine.

However, from the 1980s on, the piece of the income pie taken each year by the rich once again became as hugely disproportionate as it was in the 1920s. At the beginning of the long boom in the 1980s, the financial industry—Wall Street, brokerages, banks—accounted for around 16 percent of all American corporate profits. But by the time of last year's crash, that number had reached an incredible 41 percent.

It used to be that when our economy thrived and productivity grew, pay for working people rose accordingly. But for most of the last decade, that central piece of the American social contract simply stopped operating. People put up with it for the same reason that the great mass of losers in casinos put up with odds that favor the house. The spectacle of a few ecstatic big winners encourages the losers to believe that, hey, they might get lucky and win, too. In effect, we turned the United States into a winner-take-all casino economy, substituting the gambling hall for the factory floor as our governing economic metaphor, an assembly of anxious individual strangers whose fortunes depend overwhelmingly on random luck rather than on productive work in collective enterprises. Risk taking is fabulous, central to the American ethos—but not when it's involuntary and extreme. Too many Americans were too suddenly herded into our new national economic casino, and without debate turned into the suckers whose losses became the elite's winnings.

During the last few years, a majority of Americans came to understand that this approach wasn't working, which is why they took away control of Congress and then the White House from the Republicans in 2006 and 2008. The GOP had kept power as long as it did by pitching itself convincingly as the good-old-days party, appealing to a nostalgic hunger for the wholesome, coherent society and culture of mid-century, before life went crazy around 1968. What Obama and the Democrats did is the same thing, only different—that is, appeal to the nostalgic hunger for the sense of basic economic security and fairness that prevailed before life went crazy around 1986. Just as Republicans had for

forty years depicted Democrats as insanely freewheeling social experimenters determined to lavish money on the undeserving poor, now the caricature has been reversed: the
GOP became the party of arrogant, reckless risk takers determined to lavish money on the undeserving rich.

THREE

The Reckoning

It was the attacks of 9/11 that we supposed, at the time, had "changed everything." Except for national security, however, American life returned to normal. After the alarm went off, we punched the snooze button and drifted back to sleep, dreaming of easy money and flat-screen TVs. But now we're fully awake, and everything really has changed. Here we are, going on two years into the Great Recession, with the bottom only just barely in sight. And almost a year after the financial system began imploding, it's still iffy. The party is finally, definitely over. And the present decade, which we've never even agreed what to call—the 2000s? the aughts?—has now acquired its permanent character as a historical pivot defined by the nightmares of 9/11 and the Panic of 2008–2009. All of us, and certainly those of us old enough to remember life before our twenty-six-year-long spree began, will be spending the rest of our lives dealing with its consequences—in economics, foreign policy, culture, politics, the warp and woof of our daily lives.

During the 1980s and 1990s, we were Wile E. Coyote racing heedlessly across the endless American landscape at maximum speed. And then we spent the beginning of the twenty-first century suspended in midair just past the end of the cliff. Finally, last year, gravity reasserted itself, and we plummeted.

In the Road Runner cartoons, after each hapless crack-up the coyote always survives, and America isn't about to expire either. But unlike Wile E. Coyote, who simply keeps careening and smashing into the same spectacular dead ends, we can learn from our mistakes. We must not, I hasten to add, start behaving now like overcautious, unambitious scaredy-cats. Just as the majority in Washington believes that this is the time for big moves on health care and energy policy and immigration, it is also the moment for businesspeople to think different and think big. One or more of the three old-line American auto companies may not survive; manufacturing generally, as well as the businesses of media and retail and, of course, banking, is being fundamentally restructured. For entrepreneurs, however, this great dying off and impending void present vast opportunity.

Enthusiasts for unfettered American-style capitalism have for years blithely reminded us that the withering away of enterprises and entire industries is a healthy and necessary part of a vibrant, self-correcting economic system. Fair enough. But now, more than at any time since the economist Joseph Schumpeter popularized the idea of "creative destruction" in 1942, we are obliged to endure the shocking and awesome pain of that metamorphosis. After decades of talking the free-market talk, now we've all got to walk the walk.

We cannot just hunker down, cross our fingers, hysterically pinch our pennies, wait for the crisis to pass, and expect to go back to business as usual. All that conventional political wisdom about 2008 being a "change" year? We had no idea. Recently, Rush Limbaugh appeared on Sean Hannity's Fox News show, panicking not so much about our economic straits as about how the political winds are blowing as a result. If we now, at long last, manage to achieve something like universal health care, Limbaugh warned, it would mean "the end of America as we know it." He's right, but that's not necessarily a bad thing. This *is* the end of the world as we've known it. But it isn't the end of the world.

FOUR

The Ant, the Grasshopper, and the Rhymes of History

Remember the fable of the ant and the grasshopper? The ant is sober and disciplined, the grasshopper eats and plays and parties as if the good times will last forever—and then a killing winter descends. (In some tellings, the grasshopper dies; in some, the ant saves him.) Americans are, God bless us, energetic grasshoppers as well as energetic ants, a sui generis crossbreed, which is why we've been so successful as a nation. Our moxie comes in two basic types. On the one hand, we possess those Yankee virtues embodied by the founders: sobriety, hard work, practical ingenuity, common sense, fair play. But then there's our irrepressibly wilder, faster, and looser side, that packet of attributes that make us American instead of Canadian: impatient, hell-bent, self-invented gamblers, with a weakness for confidence games, and for blue smoke and mirrors. A certain fired-up imprudence was present from the beginning—sailing across the Atlantic in the early seventeenth century? in little wooden ships? to fashion radically new lives? in an uncharted wilderness? Crazy, man.

But it took a couple of centuries for the dreamiest, most extravagant version of the American Dream to take hold of the national imagination. The accidental discovery of gold in northern California in 1848 provoked a mad scramble by tens of thousands of ambitious fortune seekers from all over America and the world who descended on San Francisco and the nearby hills and valleys. For the first time, there were riches for the plucking by anyone, and no adult supervision. Real life briefly resembled a fairy tale.

And ever since, we Americans have been repeatedly wont to abandon prudence and the tedium of saving and building in favor of the fantastic idea that anybody, given enough pluck and luck and liberty, can make a fortune overnight. How perfect it was that in the 1990s, the freshly discovered marvels of digital technology provoked a mad scramble by tens of thousands of ambitious fortune seekers from all over America and the world who descended on San Francisco and vicinity in pursuit of the latest ultra-dreamy version of the American Dream. Of course, just as the gold rush had ended by the early 1850s, in 2000 the dot-com bubble popped. In both instances, a lucky minority had gotten rich, and most of the unfortunate majority dusted themselves off and got on with their lives. Today, once again, the bursting bubble has been bigger in northern California, with house prices dropping and foreclosures increasing far more there than in America as a whole.

The point is that while our country and our national self-perception must now change significantly, we have been here before. It's simply time to ratchet back our wild and crazy grasshopper side and get in touch with our inner ant, to be more artisan/enterpriser and less prospector/speculator, more heroic greatest generation and less self-indulgent baby boomer, to return from Oz to Kansas, to become fully reality-based once more.

And not coincidentally, just as our two-sided national character has always toggled back and forth between its steady and its skylarking aspects, so, too, does our national history run in cycles. These cyclical tides in the political zeitgeist were spotted by Ralph Waldo Emerson and Henry Adams in the nineteenth century, and by the historians Arthur Schlesinger Sr. and Jr. in the twentieth. According to the Schlesinger model, we are now at the start of the fifteenth alternating cycle since the founding of the United States, currently making yet another of our periodic shifts from an unfettered zeal for individual getting and spending to a rediscovery of the common good. The switch has flipped once again, and "the business of America is business" no longer seems inarguably true, but narrow, callous, a little crazy. It's the way our history has always unfolded, back and forth and back and forth again.

Yet in fact, according to my reading of American history, there are two interconnected but semi-independent cyclical waves, one for politics and the general national spirit, the other for economic growth and contraction. Think of the two wave systems as running along the same time line but moving perpendicular to each other, politics on the horizontal weaving right to left to right, economics on the vertical weaving up and down. Each wave system affects the other, but unpredictably, since each one has its own waxing and waning dynamic, and its own frequency.

A political or economic era can be as brief as ten or a dozen years or as long as a quarter century, but the cycles of politics and economics only occasionally fall into sync. A period of prosperity, for instance, sometimes reinforces a "natural" cyclical political shift toward the right, as it did after World War II and for most of the last twenty-five years.

But it can also accelerate a turn to the left, as it did in the early 1960s. Nor do the more democratic eras necessarily produce Democratic presidents, or vice versa. Jimmy Carter and Bill Clinton, elected during the long greed-is-good cycle, Carter near the beginning and Clinton near the end, presided over the most conservative Democratic administrations of the twentieth century. And Richard Nixon, because he was elected during the last public-spirited cycle, was by far the most liberal Republican president of our lifetimes, creating the Environmental Protection Agency, establishing relations with China, embarking on nuclear arms treaties, even instituting wage and price controls. And then there are the occasional social and cultural discombobulations provoked by a radical zig, such as the countercultural upheavals of the late 1960s and early 1970s, which can then make the zag that follows longer and more extreme, as was the case with the political period we've just passed through.

Every now and then, however, an abrupt and severe end of flush economic times happens to coincide with the natural end of a conservative political era, making the historical waves fall powerfully into sync. That's what happened in the 1930s, following three straight conservative presidencies, a period of whiz-bang technological progress—

electrification, radio, movies, automobiles, aviation—and a culture of *bon temps rouler.* And that's what's happening now.

This time around, as it happens, the waves of American political and economic history are coinciding as three huge, worldwide, and mutually reinforcing trends are also transforming the nature of the game. First, the ubiquity of networked digital devices, the constantly falling cost of digital memory, and the profusion of broadband channels— that is, the tech revolution—are transforming business and daily life. Second, during the last couple of decades, telecommunications technology and cheaper, oil-fueled travel truly and irrevocably globalized the planet. And the third big phenomenon, climate change—exacerbated by the wondrous, globalizing growth of coal- and oil-burning economies like China's and India's—is redrawing the parameters of sensible economics and politics.

We'll see soon enough how well Barack Obama copes with this perfect storm. However, even before last year's collapse of real estate prices and credit markets and Wall Street, he had a good sense of the nature of the historical moment. His Democratic opponents were all over him last year when he gave the Reagan Revolution its due, but he was exactly right. "Ronald Reagan," Obama said when he was still fighting to win the Democratic nomination, "changed the trajectory of America . . . He tapped into what people were already feeling . . . [He] transformed American politics and set the agenda for a long time . . . [I]n political terms, we may be in one of those moments where we can get a seismic shift in how the country views itself and our future. And we have to take advantage of that."

. . .

In 1941, a dozen years after the Great Depression began, Henry Luce, the co-founder of the Time-Life media empire, published an essay celebrating a national history that had "teemed with manifold projects and magnificent purposes . . . It is in this spirit," Luce wrote, "that all of us are called, each to his own measure of capacity, and each in the widest horizon of his vision, to create the first great American Century." And so we did. Indeed, for all of us alive today, "the American Century" is simply life as we know it.

The question now is how far we can extend the American heyday of manifold projects and magnificent purposes and, yes, national greatness. Golden ages and empires do come to an end. In his inaugural address, President Obama pointed to that elephant in the room—our "nagging fear that America's decline is inevitable."

"History doesn't repeat itself," Mark Twain is supposed to have said, "but it rhymes." What's happening today isn't a repetition of 1932, when the Dow Jones Industrial Average had dropped 90 percent from its peak three years earlier and the unemployment rate exceeded 23 percent. But now most definitely rhymes with then: the crash, the severe economic contraction and crisis, the graceful and inspiring new president (and First Lady), the possibility of a radical reshaping of not only our economic and financial systems but also the ways that Americans think about their country and themselves.

And there are other historical moments that also have unmistakable resonance with the present. We've just finished living through a long Gilded Age in which rich Americans got richer and more and more people began consuming conspicuously. The original Gilded Age began a century earlier, in the 1870s, during a laissez-faire boom that lasted from the end of one Wall Street and banking meltdown (the Panic of 1873) to the beginning of another (the Panic of 1893).

But there'd been earlier American financial crises—

such as the Panic of 1837, which was also triggered by New York bank failures and which, like subsequent and previous national panics, led to a severe recession. Ralph Waldo Emerson found some silver linings in the Panic of 1837 and its aftermath. "I see a good in such emphatic and universal calamity as the times bring," he wrote. "That they dissatisfy me with society." And so here we are again, with the new White House chief of staff declaring that our imploded economy and failing banks and plainly unsustainable system of health care will allow some of the rot and dysfunction to be cleared away. "You never want a serious crisis," he said, "to go to waste."

After the Panic of 1837 and the resulting recession, a booming, rollicking new era arrived that seems uncannily familiar to anyone who's been living in America for the last couple of decades.

In the 1840s, the new steamships and railroads enabled international trade and emigration to scale up as never before. Extraordinary and transformative new communications technologies suddenly appeared—not just instantaneous communication with the electric telegraph, but also instantaneous image-making with photography. Perpetually faster and cheaper printing allowed for an exponential growth of media, a lot of it scurrilous and partisan and celebrity mad. When Charles Dickens visited New York from England in 1842, he sounded like certain old fogies disgusted by the blogosphere and Twittering a century and a half later, horrified by the spectacle of "fifty newspapers . . . pimping and pandering for all degrees of vicious taste, and . . . imputing to every man in public life the coarsest and the vilest motives." A subculture known as the Bowery B'hoys preceded hip-hop by 130 years—a self-conscious youth style that arose spontaneously in the poor neighborhoods of New York City, rude and stylish, glorifying sex and violence, creating its own language and its own fashions, and finding its own new forms of entertainment. Modern marketing was essentially born in the 1840s, including the first department stores, the first advertising agencies, the first presidential campaigns in which marketers re-branded upper-class candidates as rustic men of the people.

There was also a nature-worshipping backlash to the manic new era of growth and materialism and self-congratulation. Henry David Thoreau was off in the woods, starting to write his essay *Walden,* laying the groundwork for everything we know today as the green dream. "I delight to come to my bearings," Thoreau wrote, "not to live in this restless, nervous, bustling, trivial Nineteenth Century, but stand or sit thoughtfully while it goes by." In the 1840s, various Christian sects were predicting imminent Armageddon, the end of mankind and civilization. In 1846, the United States invaded a foreign nation for the first time—a desert country (Mexico, not Iraq) that had a natural resource we needed (land, not oil) and that the president (James K. Polk, not George W. Bush) insisted was an imminent military threat to the United States.

And America in 2009 also looks as if it might rhyme, uncomfortably, with Great Britain circa 1909. A hundred years ago, the British were coming off a proud century as the most important nation on earth—economically, politically, militarily, culturally. But the United States was coming on fast, having already overtaken the mother country economically (in per capita gross domestic product), and about to do so on all the other major axes of national power and influence. The United States surpassed the United Kingdom in the twentieth century for many reasons: a much larger area and population, fewer fetters on individual gumption, a younger nation's ability to make faster social and economic turns. Between the beginning of World War I and the end of World War II, as America emerged as the unequivocal world leader, Great Britain became an admirable also-ran, still significant but radically diminished as a global player. Applying that template to the twenty-first century, China would be the new us—feverish with individual and national drive, manufacturer to the world, growing like crazy, bigger and much more populous than the reigning superpower. And thus our next half century would, according to this analogy, unfold like Britain's in the first half of the twentieth century, requiring an extreme new humility as we reduce our national ambitions and self-conception.

One can imagine far worse American scenarios than becoming a supersized Great Britain. But even that diminution isn't certain. Historical destinies are directional, not precisely preordained. As I say, history tends to rhyme, not repeat. To a great extent, our national future will unfold over this century according to the collective and individual choices we make now.

FIVE

Change Is Possible

We've brought about the current crises through a quarter century of self-destructive financial excess and reckless overdependence on debt and fossil fuels. Yet during the same quarter century we've become familiar with a clear-eyed and often effective way of thinking about self-destructive excess and unhealthy dependence. In other words, the vocabulary of addiction recovery might come in handy. We've just had two two-term presidents who publicly struggled to overcome addictions (to sex and booze, respectively), and as a nation we are substance abusers coming off a long bender, now hitting bottom (we can only hope). I've always thought some of the Twelve Steps were superfluous, so here is a streamlined, secularized Seven-Step Program for America—Bubbleholics Anonymous?—to start getting back on track:

- *Admit that we were powerless over addiction to easy money and cheap fossil fuel and living large.*
- *Believe that we can, individually and collectively, re-store ourselves to sanity and normal living.*
- *Make a searching and fearless moral inventory of our-selves.*
- *Admit the exact nature of our wrongs.*
- *Be entirely ready to remove our defects of character.*
- *Seek to improve our awareness of law and of the nat-ural forces that govern life, hoping only for knowledge of right and wrong and the strength to follow that knowledge.*
- *Having had an awakening as the result of these steps, try to carry this message and to practice these princi-ples in all our affairs.*

Of course, we all know that when addicts finally man-age to quit, they feel awful for a while, and that's where we are right now. This last year of recession, provoked by the sudden, essentially cold-turkey abandonment of spend-ing, lending, and borrowing, is something like our na-tional equivalent of the jitters, sweats, goose bumps, and seizures that addicts experience right after they give up their junk. In fact, though, the applicable addiction trope is more like food or sex than drugs or alcohol, since as economic creatures we cannot simply quit. Instead, we have to teach ourselves to buy and sell and borrow in healthier, more moderate ways. The new America must be about financial temperance, not abstinence.

Our great national rehab won't be easy. But it wasn't only in olden times that Americans successfully coped with breathtaking flux and undertook dramatic change. In fact, without quite realizing what we were doing, *we just did it.* Consider all that's happened during the era that ended last year, and to which we adjusted rather easily, given the scale and rapidity of the changes.

Until the 1980s, we had one telephone company and four big national television channels. Now we've adapted to hundreds of TV channels and multiple phone companies, as well as airlines and health insurance entities that arise and disappear as fast as strip-mall stores. Pornography is universally and easily available, and pretty much everyone, since HIV/AIDS emerged, has learned to use condoms. And we've grown accustomed to the weird transparency, instant accessibility, and 24/7 connectedness of the new digital world.

The other transformations America has undergone

since the early 1980s are no less drastic for being unam-
biguously positive:

- *Back then, half again as many of us smoked cigarettes.*
- *We have sequenced the human genome.*
- *We watched (and helped) the Soviet Union and its
  European empire collapse, and watched (and helped)
  China change from a backward, impoverished, danger-
  ous Orwellian nation into a booming, much less
  Orwellian member of the civilized global order.*
- *We've managed to reduce murder in New York City by
  two-thirds and crime almost everywhere by unthink-
  able amounts.*
- *Women have come close to achieving true equality of
  expectations and opportunity.*
- *Being gay has become astoundingly public and unre-
  markable.*
- *We've elected a black president.*

In other words, as a society we remain flexible, nimble, still
able to enact and adapt to dramatic change. This time
around, though, compared with the early 1980s, when the
last long political and economic era began, it's much

clearer from the get-go that one epoch has ended and a new one is about to begin. A lot of the change that's necessary now must be the result of deliberate policy choices, as we reconsider the habits and schemes that got us into this mess and remake our systems accordingly. But at least as much of the refashioned new America will be the result of transformed attitudes and sensibility, changes in our understandings of what's important and sensible and attractive, and what feels hollow or silly or nuts.

SIX

The Shape of Things to Come

The reset button has been pushed. So what will be the protocols and look and feel of the America about to emerge?

The Revival of Pragmatism

A primary reason for Barack Obama's election and his high approval ratings as president is his privileging of the empirical and pragmatic ahead of ideological reflex. We have not, of course, arrived in a golden age of fair-minded, intellectually honest post-partisanship, as party-line congressional votes and the brain-dead professional partisans' redoubled ferocity prove. But a majority of Americans out in America are dialing back or turning off their ideological autopilots. Despite decades of red-versus-blue divisiveness and, since the inauguration, the hysterical anti-Obama propagandizing, in a CBS News/*New York Times* poll last spring fully 37 percent of Republicans and 72 percent of independents who registered an opinion said they approved of Obama's performance as president. This is thanks in part to Obama's personnel and policy decisions and approach, and in part to the extremity of the economic and financial emergencies we face. (There may be no atheists in foxholes, but there are not too many ideologues, either.)

It's also due to the post–Cold War realities finally and fully sinking in. With the Soviet Union gone and China socialist in name only, the specter of communism is no longer haunting us, so programmatic whiffs of "socialism" are not remotely as toxic politically as they used to be. Republicans have been getting little political traction with their insistence, before and after his election, that Obama is a socialist. That bogeyman pretty much wore itself out at the end of the last century, and these days reliably frightens only people desperate for simple black-and-white understandings of the way the world works. Rather, it's now capitalist piggishness more than collectivism that provokes genuine and widespread fear and loathing. When half of the Republicans in the House of Representatives vote for a confiscatory 90 percent tax on Wall Street executives' incomes, as they did earlier this year, the old "class warfare" lines seem moot.

Ideological thinking is not over, as Daniel Bell suggested it was in 1960 (*The End of Ideology*) and Francis Fukuyama more grandly reasserted in 1992 (*The End of History and the Last Man*). But the familiar old polarities of right and left are happily losing their salience. For a while at least, America will be in a state of ideological flux, which should free us, as we haven't been free for most of a century, to improvise a fresh course forward.

For instance, the powerful and obvious but weirdly un-made "conservative" case for universal health coverage can now be argued successfully—the idea being that if we protect every American against the mammoth downside economic risk of serious illness or accident, we will thereby empower people to accept constructive economic risks, let-ting them feel as free as possible to take new jobs and start new careers or new businesses. And if people on the left will grant that competition from charter schools (or even tax-supported private schools) could actually improve American education, then perhaps people on the right will grant that real competition in health care, from a public health-insurance plan as well as genuinely unfettered private medicine, could actually improve American health care. In other words, we could have something like guaranteed universal health coverage *and* public schools freed from the often stultifying grip of teachers' unions.

Radical pragmatism can transform our energy and environmental habits as well. During the last couple of decades in the United States, we have increased our use of gasoline by about a third, while Germany and nuclear-powered France have managed to cut their oil consumption by a quarter—which is to say, modern, wealthy societies really can move away from their overdependence on oil. We can make fossil fuels expensive enough so that solar and wind become more economical, and at the same time commit seriously to green nuclear power. Already pragmatists in the environmental movement are supporting heretofore heretical solutions such as large-scale solar-power-generating facilities and the development of technologies to reduce pollutants from coal-fired electric plants.

Similarly, we can frankly admit our egregious post-9/11 excesses in fighting Islamic terrorism—we discovered they were dangerous, and we panicked for two or three years—but we can also forgo the bloody-minded prosecutorial impulse to hunt down and punish every American who thought he was doing his best to protect the country. We can grow the armed forces and fight all necessary wars but meanwhile get rid of unaffordable pork-barrel weapons systems. Robert Gates, the secretary of defense in both the Bush and the Obama administrations, is a living exemplar of this new, post-party-line approach. And what he said about the proposed 2010 Pentagon budget—that it's "one of those rare chances to match virtue to necessity, to critically and ruthlessly separate appetites from real requirements"—is true of vast swaths of public policy right now.

The old disagreements about government intervention won't disappear, and we'll continue to have reflexive true believers on the left and the right. But with the economy now in uncharted territory, people understand that unbudging adherence to old political convictions won't provide any easy way out. Hyperbolic rants and rigid talking points, in either Limbaughian or Olbermannian flavors, now seem worse than useless, unpleasant artifacts of a bumptious barroom age. Whether or not Obama's policies are perfectly correct, his preternatural cool and reasonableness are what a large majority of Americans want and need right now, and will help define the new zeitgeist.

In politics and in life, babies do occasionally get thrown out with the bathwater, as we just discovered to be the case with the deregulatory frenzy unleashed in the 1980s. But the next new America that's about to hatch will not be some Bizarro World, where we do the opposite of everything we did during the last quarter century. History proceeds dialectically: that is, Big Idea Y eclipses Big Idea X, but only for a while, until an X + Y hybrid arises, and so on, back and forth, over and over.

The New Deal era ended, but its basic social and economic underpinnings have endured ever since. Notwithstanding the powerful backlash against the 1960s, the changes born of the era's sharp left turn—civil rights, feminism, gay rights, environmentalism, sex, drugs, rock and roll—became part of the American way of life. In the same way, even as we now rediscover the need for sensible regulation and systemic fairness, the fundamentally good lessons of the Reagan age—the free market mostly unbound, the wisdom of crowds, cheerful national pride—will endure. We will be careful not to throw too many babies out with the bathwater. The Obama administration is going out of its way, for instance, to avoid nationalizing failed banks and failing automobile companies. "We're all Keynesians now," Richard Nixon frankly admitted in 1971, near the end of the last liberal interventionist era. Today, as the subsequent era ends, it's clear that we're now all Reaganites as well. Learning from one's mistakes doesn't require a wholesale rejection of everything that came before.

Global Realism

From the 1980s on, America incrementally cured itself of its Vietnam Syndrome, our traumatized and extreme disinclination to use military power overseas: first the invasion of Grenada (1983), then the Gulf War (1991), intervention in the Balkans (1993–1995), and the defeat of the Taliban in Afghanistan (2001). But our painful Iraqi misadventure has taught us, in what feels like just the right measure, the dangers of international hubris and overreach. Iraq is not the debacle that it was two and three years ago; something sufficiently like victory now seems plausible. And so we are not, thankfully, sinking into some freshly traumatized, paralyzing Iraq Syndrome—more troops are headed for Afghanistan, after all. But we are definitely at the end of the end of Vietnam Syndrome. The pendulum has swung back to something like a sensible middle position.

The utterly international nature of our present economic hell has made it all the scarier. But in the long run I think there will be an upside, too: the meltdown amounts to a spectacular moment of global consciousness, this generation's version of the Apollo astronauts' 1968 photograph of the earth from the moon, an unforgettable reminder that all 6.7 billion of us—from Reykjavík to Sacramento, Vladivostok to Athens, Wall Street to Tiananmen—are in this together, deeply and inextricably interdependent. (The sublime always has a bit of terror mixed in.) In particular for Americans, it represents a salutary slap-in-the-face realization that China and we have effectively become a merged economic leviathan, what the historian Niall Ferguson calls "Chimerica."

Just as Obama had a sense of where we needed to steer before he was elected, so did George W. Bush back in 2000. "If we're an arrogant nation," candidate Bush said of his foreign policy vision, "they'll resent us. If we're a humble nation, but strong, they'll welcome us . . . Our nation stands alone right now . . . in terms of power. And that's why we've got to be humble . . . One way for us to end up being viewed as the Ugly American is for us to go around the world saying, 'We do it this way, so should you.' "

In this new age, we need to be confident but not crazily overconfident, proud but not boastful, daring but not . . . dicks. This country has always had an iffy relationship with humility. President John Quincy Adams was a founding imperialist. "North America," he said, is "destined by Divine Providence to be peopled by one nation." But as an older man, he also warned against imperial overreach: "America does not go abroad in search of monsters to destroy."

So now we are faced with a paradoxical, almost oxymoronic national challenge: to operate as a superpower with humility and magnanimity. The right choice is neither a bullying America-rules moralism nor a weenie-ish blame-America moralism. Rather, it's to temper our longstanding sense of righteous superiority with our equally hardwired matter-of-factness—to maintain a clear-eyed view of what's practical and sensible, to avoid believing our own bullshit.

The New New Economy

If you want to feel encouraged about our economic near future—not this damned decade but the teens—go talk to some venture capitalists. They aren't quite giddy (after the '80s, '90s, and '00s, beware all giddiness), but they do sound optimistic about an imminent tide of innovations in information technology, energy, and transportation. Recall, please, the national mood in the 1970s: after the 1960s party, we found ourselves in a slough of despond, with an oil crisis, a terrible recession, declining productivity, a kind of Weimarish embrace of cultural decadence, national malaise. And yet at that very dispirited moment, Federal Express, Microsoft, and Apple were all founded. Even now Apple and Amazon and Google have been doing better than the rest of the economy. The next transformative, moneymaking technologies and businesses are coming soon to a garage near you.

Plenty of quintessentially twentieth-century businesses that have been sickening will now, finally, die. A generation or two of managers in those industries coasted along in denial, behaving as if the dark horizon would remain perpetually a ways off. With this recession, many of them are arriving at the abyss. However, people will still want to buy cars, still need to buy houses, still want to read quality journalism, watch TV series and movies at home, listen to recorded music, and all the rest. And so starting now, as some of the huge, dominant, old-growth trees of our economic forest fall, the seedlings and saplings—that is, the people determined to produce and sell new kinds of transportation and housing and media and other merchandise in new, economically rational ways—will have a clearer field in which to grow.

The implosion of Wall Street is already having this salutary effect, prompting some bankers to start up new financial firms and others to go to work for smaller, no-name companies. Which should, among other things, help reduce the overconcentration of capital and risk that made the present crisis so dangerous and devastating. "If the risk taking spreads out to these smaller institutions, it is no longer a systemic threat," according to Matthew Richardson, a finance professor at New York University. "And innovation is spreading out too. This is a good thing."

GM and Chrysler may be on their last legs—but small, visionary American start-up companies like Aptera Motors, Fisker Automotive, Tesla Motors, and Bright Automotive are starting to sell their cool, cutting-edge battery-powered cars, and a decade from now any one of them might be the household name that epitomizes our twenty-first-century industrial rebirth. (I just drove in an Aptera. It looks like an awesome *Jetsons* vehicle, plugs into the wall, drives like a dream, goes a hundred miles on a charge, costs under $30,000—and I want one.)

Money ≠ Happiness

The ecology of business and employment at the high end is already being transformed by the Wall Street crash. That is, the definitive end of the maniacal boom in the financial industry means that careers manipulating money will no longer be so seductive to such a disproportionate share of our best and brightest. Among the 2007 graduates of Harvard College who went straight to work, about half—and fully 58 percent of the men—took jobs in finance or consulting. And it wasn't because that's the life's work they all dreamed of doing. In a survey of the members of the class of 2008, *The Harvard Crimson* asked, hypothetically, what jobs the graduates would be taking if money were not an issue: without the enormous pay disparities, half the kids heading to banks and consultancies said they'd be embarking on different career paths, and the 20 percent of the class of 2008 who went straight to work in public service, politics, the arts, and publishing would have been 39 percent instead. In the post-bubble economy, plenty of smart and ambitious young people will still pursue financial careers, and good for them. But other fields will get a bigger share of the cream, and surely more Americans will aim to do work that makes them happy rather than merely well-to-do.

For my public radio program, *Studio 360*, we've been finding and interviewing American adults who have, in these tough times, switched careers, leaving jobs that earned them good salaries in order to pursue their abiding passions.

In Tacoma, after Rohn Amegatcher's construction management firm went belly up last summer, he decided that what he really loves to do is cook and make things out of wood—and now he spends half his time preparing meals for residents of an old people's home and half his time producing one-of-a-kind furniture pieces he crafts from scrap wood and sells in galleries. LaKeisha Sabol sold real estate in Dayton, but now she lives in Las Vegas, where she's getting a degree in theater management and has worked for Cirque du Soleil, all in pursuit of her dream to create local American culturepaloozas along the lines of the Edinburgh Festival Fringe. Since losing her investment bank job, Christine Marchuska has become a fashion designer, making and selling stylish, eco-conscious women's clothes. And in suburban New York City, Marc Solomon had worked as a trial lawyer for big insurance companies for decades; after he was laid off last year, he studied sound design and started his own recording company.

Not all people have the wherewithal—financial or

personal—to forge new careers or follow their bliss in moneymaking ways. The post-bubble, post-crash dislocation and pain will be irremediable for many people. But multiply those hopeful starting-over stories by a hundred thousand or a million, and you'll have a sense of how, in the new America, necessity can be the mother of reinvention.

Older and (Maybe, Finally) Wiser

The baby boomers were historically fortunate: they missed the Great Depression and World War II, and although they grew up with the hideous ambient hum of potential nuclear Armageddon, until they reached middle age, the only great national trauma was the one—the 1960s and Vietnam—in which they were the self-regarding stars. (Compared with World War II, only a tenth as many Americans, proportionately, died in Vietnam.) After achieving generational consciousness as a hedonistic, freedom-worshipping mob of Peter Pans—*May you stay . . . forever young*—many of the boomers aged but never quite grew up.

Think about it. Back in 1963 and 1964, when I was nine years old, my friends and I were all atwitter about the first *X-Men* comic book, the new G.I. Joe action figure, and the Beatles—plus *Star Trek* was being created. At home

I wore blue jeans and sneakers, unlike my father or any other grown-up I knew, and for my birthday I wanted a set of Mattel walkie-talkies.

Now, almost half a century later, American adults are paying to see new *X-Men, G.I. Joe,* and *Star Trek* movies; this year Paul McCartney was the headliner at the Coachella music festival and a new George Harrison album was released. At home I wear jeans and sneakers, like most other grown-ups, and for my birthday I got a new iPhone. Computers and GPS devices are what we have today instead of Etch Λ Sketches and Erector sets and Morse-code telegraph kits. When I was young, anything small and plastic that had buttons and beeped was a toy; now it's some essential gadget, a thing as quintessentially grown-up as a briefcase or a bottle of Scotch used to be. Themed leisure (Disneyland, then Ronald McDonald, and finally Chuck E. Cheese) was invented in the 1950s, 1960s, and 1970s purely as children's entertainment, but since the 1980s fantasy environments for adults—the Hard Rock Cafe, Burning Man, half of Las Vegas—have taken over.

Adults of my parents' generation did not bicycle, roller-skate, or play army; adults today spend whole weekends mountain biking, snowboarding, and dressing up in camouflage gear to fire paint balls at each other. What are SUVs but enormous fantasy toys? As children we watched *Combat!* and *The Rat Patrol* and *Roy Rogers;* as adults we get to drive Jeeps and Expeditions and Land Rovers. When did Halloween become a holiday celebrated by childless adults? When did Americans over twelve start eating Pop-Tarts? Ice cream used to be a kiddie treat, but beginning with adults of the Ben & Jerry's generation it has become a central form of self-pampering, a kind of kids-are-us sacrament. Until adults became devoted to chocolate-chip-cookie-dough ice cream, no manufacturer would have dared produce a product as exquisitely, childishly indulgent—just as it took Steven Spielberg and George Lucas and their followers in Hollywood to invent a new genre, live-action kids' entertainment good and lavish enough to appeal to adults.

In the 1960s, I would have been creeped out to meet a grown-up who read *Fantastic Four* or *Batman,* but of course in the 1980s and 1990s it was adults who drove the comic-book boom, and who buy most video games today. For my parents, animation was not appointment television. Today, adults watch *South Park* and read the Harry Potter novels without embarrassment. It can't be coincidence that a majority of the celebrated younger American visual artists have worked most famously in neo-kiddie media—Julian Schnabel's broken crockery, Keith Haring's notebook doodles, Jeff Koons's nursery-school tchotchkes, Cindy Sherman's spook-house dress-up photographs.

After backpacks became faddish among schoolboys and schoolgirls, they also became de rigueur for fashionable women. One female professional I know wears a Curious George backpack, and another buys clothes for herself out of her daughters' Hanna Andersson catalog. Why did grown-ups start wearing sweat suits in public? Why did chinos and jeans and polo shirts replace suits and ties in the office? Because our mothers stopped dressing us—and who wouldn't rather stay in play clothes all day long? In the coolest offices, especially on the West Coast, they don't just dress like kids; they actually stock the places with toys and games, Slinkys and Mr. Potato Heads, Foosball and Halo. These days, if you want to ask someone how the job is going, even if she's a deputy attorney general or a CFO, the standard form of the question is "Are you having fun?"

Waiting a while to get everything you want is—or anyhow was—a definition of maturity. Demanding satisfaction right this instant, on the other hand, is a defining behavior of seven-year-olds. The most powerful appeal of the Web is not the "community" it enables but its instantaneity: for better or worse, you can send a message *now*, get any question answered *now*, pick your airline seat *now*, buy anything you want right *now*. Cell phones and the Internet, together with FedEx and UPS, finally and fully satisfy the permanent child within each of us—the impulsive child with zero tolerance for waiting. And as a result, during the last quarter century, delayed gratification itself came to seem quaint and unnecessary.

This is not meant as a condemnation of maximizing fun and living casually. I am committed to wearing rubber-soled shoes, watching *The Simpsons*, and making back-of-the-classroom wisecracks on Twitter. But the rampant juvenilization of national life can echo and reinforce unfortunate habits of mind. What do the naughtiest children do? They scream and cry and exaggerate, like Glenn Beck. What do we tell nice children about their ugly scribbles and cockamamy ideas and pointless stories? That they're all just great, no better or worse than any other child's—which, carried full strength into the adult world, becomes an undiscriminating hyper-empathy, where Alice Walker is an important novelist and Mitch Albom a great spiritual guide. Who have been this recent era's religious superstars, the subjects of best-selling nonfiction books, TV series, prayers for intercession? *Angels.* A lot of today's adults apparently never got over discovering the awful truth about Santa Claus.

The postwar generation was the first to refuse to grow up, but Gen X and the rest have followed in those footsteps. And the selfish, heedless, if-it-feels-good-do-it approach enshrined by young boomers subsequently enabled the risk-taking, party-hearty paradigm that has governed so much of American life, economically and otherwise, for the last quarter century. Now, in the twilight of their hegemony, with this crisis and the necessary reshaping of America, the boomers have their last best shot at helping to straighten out the mess they helped to make. In their empty-nest years, for instance, perhaps they can channel some of the vast energies and micromanagement they lavished on their children to pro-social enterprises and volunteer work.

On the other hand, the so-called millennials—the children and grandchildren of the boomers—have come of age during a period defined by the digital revolution, globalization, 9/11, a pair of ambiguous and difficult but not wholly disastrous wars, two financial bubbles bursting, a possible depression, and the election (*their* election, in their not unreasonable view) of an African-American president. All in all, it seems to me, these are probably the makings of a healthier, more useful generational creation myth than the assassinations, antiwar protests, and countercultural bacchanalia of the 1960s and early 1970s. The millennials' manifest tendency toward consensus, common sense, and libertarian tolerance equips them well for the new age. Teach for America, the private program that sends new college graduates into poor schools for two-year teaching stints, had a 42 percent increase in applications this year, to thirty-five thousand—including, remarkably, one out of nine Ivy League seniors. In other words, the kids are all right, and if they can keep their instant-access sense of entitlement in check, they just might turn out to be the next greatest generation.

Equality for Real

On the unequivocal plus side, of course, baby boomers also made up most of the cohort who waged and enabled and won (or capitulated to) the feminist revolution. As recently as two years ago, the Department of Labor was projecting that not until 2016 would the female proportion of the labor force reach 47 percent. But that was then; the future has arrived early. Because more than eight out of ten workers laid off in this recession have been men, women now suddenly constitute a majority of American workers. It seems plausible to imagine that as a result the ways we think about and organize work will evolve a bit faster now: less of an unemotional command-and-control ethos, more flexibility to juggle work and family life, telecommuting even more common. And in the society at large, the idea of gender equality should become more entrenched.

A year ago, we thought we just might be on the verge of a remarkable moment—a milestone of racial progress, thanks to the possible election of Barack Obama. It is bizarre how secondary (hell, tertiary) that profound change now seems. It's as if Jesus had returned—and then a few days later extraterrestrials landed, so as a result everybody stopped paying much attention to the holy dude. But it's also a perfectly apt and gratifying turn of events. As a candidate, Obama positioned himself as a smart, steady character who happened to be black, and the economic emergency that ensured his election has now pushed the fact of his race and its heavy symbolic freight into the shadows of public consciousness. Once the present crises have passed, however, I think we will rediscover the ramifications, small and large, of the astonishingly enlightened national turn we made last November 4, and begin enjoying the fruits of a new era of racial reconciliation.

Sustainability in Every Sense

Whether or not Congress passes some kind of carbon tax or cap-and-trade scheme that ushers in a true alternative-energy era (before the inevitably rising price of oil forces our panicky hand five or ten years from now), "sustainability" is going to be shaping individual and public policy decisions. And I don't just mean recycling trash, driving more fuel-efficient cars, and using compact fluorescent lightbulbs. Annual increases of 10 and 15 percent in real estate prices were not sustainable. Endlessly lowering taxes and expanding government isn't sustainable. Our system of health care and "the war on drugs" as currently constituted are not sustainable. Sustainability in this sense is as much old-fashioned green-eyeshade Republicanism as it is newfangled "Kumbaya"-ish green talk, and achieving it will require partisans on both sides to face facts and make unpleasant choices.

Yes, we must start spending again, and we will. But like those people who, having survived the 1930s, never entirely lost their Depression-born habits of frugality, we survivors of 2008 and 2009, one hopes, will be chastened. The Chinese regime may not want us to start behaving more like the Chinese people, by spending less and saving more ("it is not the right time" for Americans to become fiscally prudent, the head of China's central bank had the gall to say last spring), but of course we must.

Even after the economy recovers, deciding to forgo that fancy new house or third TV or bigger car or marginally sexier laptop will come more naturally. The third of Americans who struggle economically will continue to struggle. But the fortunate majority of us—those of us with jobs, with some savings, with incomes that let us make ends meet—are already discovering that living within one's means doesn't necessarily diminish quality of life. In fact, dialing down the money madness and material envy and acquisitiveness—finally getting over the 1980s fever—can actually make us feel better. Some of the best things in life really are free, or at least inexpensive.

We don't need to turn ourselves into tedious zero-body-fat, zero-carbon-footprint ascetics. But who do you think enjoys life more, Donald Trump or Warren Buffett? They are both symbols of the era just ended, but one is a clownish reality-show artifact living the high life in Manhattan and Palm Beach and the other a respected and beloved avatar who lives in a modest house in Omaha and has already donated most of his fortune to charity.

Building Real Communities

The housing industry remains comatose, but even that has a silver lining. We thus have a moment to pause and reflect before we begin building again. Are new houses today three times as gratifying as our parents' and grandparents' houses were back in the day? Surely not, even though we inhabit three times as much house per person as we did in 1950. And when big-time real estate development finally does resume, perhaps we can contrive to make more of it happen smartly, wisely. We could finally move beyond the helter-skelter, anything-goes approach of the postwar era, and instead start creating more coherent, walkable, pleasant towns and cities along the lines of the old-fashioned places everyone instinctively loves—cozy, carefully designed real towns instead of generic sprawl, Coral Gables instead of Orlando, new San Franciscos rather than more San Fernando Valleys—in other words, retrofitted neighborhoods and new developments designed to become true communities. Urban planning can be our friend, if we acquire the political will to use it. "The days where we're just building sprawl forever," President Obama said recently at a town hall meeting in south Florida, "those days are over. I think that Republicans, Democrats—everybody recognizes that that's not a smart way to design communities."

Fun and Creativity

Although certain self-parodying epiphenomena of the Age of Excess—*so long, Paris Hilton!*—are about to disappear, fun will endure. Irony is not dead. Hollywood is doing fantastic box-office business, 15 percent more this year than last, thanks to fantastically frivolous movies like *Paul Blart: Mall Cop, Madea Goes to Jail, Fast & Furious,* and *The Hangover. The Daily Show* and *The Colbert Report* have been special havens of sanity amid last year's sky-is-falling hysteria. And again, history is encouraging in this regard: *Saturday Night Live* and modern comedy were born during the malaise-y 1970s, just as a great germinal moment of wit and humor—*The New Yorker,* the Marx Brothers, screwball comedy—flourished during the depressed 1930s.

I'm even hopeful that the meltdown and resulting reset might jar the culture and its makers in deeper ways. For the last three decades, too much of art and design and entertainment has seemed caught in a kind of automatic, mindless historical-revival cul-de-sac, almost compulsively recycling styles and remaking and remixing the greatest hits of the past. (Think postmodern architecture, pop music based on sampling, 1960s-style dresses, pseudo-mid-century home decor, movies about twentieth-century superheroes.) Since we're now finished with twenty-five- or thirty-year-long eras in both politics and economics, maybe a new, post-nostalgic cultural epoch will emerge as well. Maybe the new fiscal restraint itself will summon up creative innovation and excellence. "Starting about six months ago," a Hollywood agent told *The Wall Street Journal* last spring, "the [movie] studios started to make a unified and determined effort to cut back" on insanely overgenerous deals for superstar actors and directors. "They're just not going to keep losing vast amounts of money while paying out millions to the first-dollar-gross players." Maybe more of the next big things in movies and theater and music and architecture and design will be actually, thrillingly *new*.

SEVEN

Keys to Renewal

In this new era Americans will surely have to adjust the ways we think of ourselves. Still an exceptional country, absolutely, but not a magical one exempt from the laws of economic and geopolitical gravity. A nation with plenty of mojo, sure, but in our third century informed by the traditional wisdom of middle age a little more than the pedal-to-the-metal madness of youth.

The same goes for our individual senses of entitlement. During the perma-'80s, way too many of us were operating, consciously or not, with a dreamy gold-rush vision of getting rich the day after tomorrow and then cruising along as members of an impossibly large leisure class. (That was always the yuppie dream: an aristocratic life-style achieved meritocratically.) Now that our long era of self-enchantment has ended, however, each of us, gob-smacked and reality-checked by the harrowing new circumstances, is recalibrating expectations for the timing and scale of our particular version of the good life.

However, even though most of our hypothetical individual futures don't look quite so deluxe, as a nation we have three special strengths that, managed correctly and given a little luck, could allow America to remain at the top of the heap for a long time to come.

Immigration

No other nation on earth assimilates immigrants as successfully as the United States. There are those who argue that we can no longer afford to open our doors so wide, but in fact precisely the opposite is true. Beyond giving sentimental, self-flattering lip service to our history as "a nation of immigrants," the sooner we can agree on a coherent and correctly self-serving national immigration policy—that is, to encourage and enable as many as possible of the world's smartest and most hardworking and open-minded people to become Americans—the better our chances of forestalling national decline.

I recently asked a friend of mine who operates a large farming business in California how many of his hundreds of employees are undocumented Mexican immigrants. "Ninety percent," he told me. I literally gasped. And such numbers are not unique to agriculture or to California. Just as we are now dependent on cheap credit and cheap manufactured goods from China, we really can't afford to say no to cheap laborers from Mexico and Central America, and we need to admit that truth and make the system for absorbing them rational. At the upper end of the scale, it's crazily self-defeating for us to set arbitrary and entirely politicized limits on the visas we grant to skilled foreign workers, such as software engineers and nurses. Wouldn't it make more sense to establish a politically independent federal apparatus, like the Federal Reserve System, that would adjust immigration quotas according to the actual and projected ebbs and flows of our economy? The waves of exotic foreigners who poured in during the nineteenth and early twentieth centuries were unsettling to Americans at the time—culturally, economically, and politically. But our forebears got over it, fortunately, since the newcomers were instrumental in forging the American Century.

Technology

For most of the last two hundred years, a great driver of our national prosperity and power was the extraordinary physical scale of our land, our natural resources, and our population, the more the better—a mostly empty continent ripe for exploitation and settlement, vast deposits of essential industrial matériel, many millions of laborers to build new cities from scratch and operate Brobdingnagian assembly lines turning out steel and automobiles and aircraft. China has similar advantages today, and partly because we (and the rest of the developed world) have already been there and done that, paving the way, they've been able to develop in fast motion, cramming a hundred years of development into the last thirty.

But I'm reminded of Philip Johnson's apt, bitchy description of Frank Lloyd Wright during the modernist, forward-looking 1930s "as the greatest architect of the 19th century." China today is the greatest country of the twentieth century. Muscular industrialism gets you only so far. In the twenty-first century, further increases in productivity and prosperity require ingenuity and enterprise applied at the micro scale—digital devices and systems, fantastic new technical materials, biotechnology, subatomic nanotechnology. As China and other developing countries finally achieve the industrial plenty that we enjoyed fifty and a hundred years ago, the United States can, instead of grieving over the demise of Detroit, once again pioneer the new, next-generation technologies that the increasingly industrialized world will require.

Optimizing immigration and new technologies requires policy choices born of a new collective wisdom that must be expressed politically. But exploiting our third great American legacy is almost entirely up to each of us, as individuals.

The Amateur Spirit

It was our unthinking trust in the unthinking certainty of professionals and experts that helped get us into this mess: *securitized debt? credit default swaps? uh, sure, whatever.* The crisis should therefore prompt Americans now to call upon the old-fashioned, self-reliant, enthusiastic, commonsensical part of themselves—that is, their amateur spirit.

This nation, after all, was created by passionate amateurs. The American spirit really *is* the amateur spirit. The earliest settlers were amateur colonists. "I see democracy," the historian Daniel Boorstin wrote twenty years ago, as "government by amateurs, as a way of confessing the limits of our knowledge." In the early nineteenth century, Alexis de Tocqueville approvingly noted the absence of "public careers" in America—that is, the rarity of professional politicians. Back then, "amateur" was an entirely positive, noble, virtuous description of someone. An amateur pursuit meant something that one pursued—a field of study, an artistic enterprise, a craft—not unseriously, but out of passion rather than merely to earn a living. The Latin root is *amator*, or "lover."

Benjamin Franklin's profession was printing, but he made history as an amateur—an amateur scientist and inventor, an amateur politician leading the way to national independence and crafting the Constitution. Thomas Jefferson was a professional lawyer, but it was as an amateur political philosopher that he wrote the Declaration of Independence, and as an amateur architect that he designed Monticello, one of the great, defining American buildings.

For most of the last century, however, it was all downhill for the reputation of the amateur impulse. "Amateur" came to be a pejorative. According to *The American Heritage Dictionary*, an amateur is "one lacking professional skill or ease in a certain area, as in art," and as an adjective means "unskillful." A kind of tyranny of professionalism arose.

Of course, just as there's good cholesterol and bad cholesterol, there's good professionalism and bad professionalism. Good professionalism means competence, conscientiousness, and accountability. Bad professionalism consists in being arrogant about having the right answers, paying more attention to credentials than talent, automatically opposing new ideas, defaulting to jargon.

"The amateur," by contrast, Boorstin wrote, "is not afraid to do something for the first time . . . [T]he rewards and refreshments of thought and the arts come from the courage to try something, all sorts of things, for the first time. An enamored amateur need not be a genius to stay out of the ruts he has never been trained in." Amateurs are passionate. They do the things they want to do in the ways they want to do them. They don't worry too much about breaking rules and aren't paralyzed by a fear of imperfection or even failure. They embrace new challenges. And it's that attitude, infusing our occupations as much as possible with the joy and excitement of avocation, that will get us through this wrenching time of creative destruction, confusion, and change.

Happily, one of the by-products of these heady last fifteen years has been a renaissance, still spreading widely and deeply, of America's traditional, tinkering amateur spirit. The Internet and the Web were originally the products of vision and ingenuity, not moneymaking monomania, and the open-source movement in software and homemade content online carry on that animating impulse, transforming technology and commerce and the culture. Thanks to the do-it-yourself empowerment of new digital tools, thousands of people are blogging and publishing, making films and videos and music, creating useful and entertaining Web sites and applications. It's the amateur spirit run wild, and if we're lucky, it will be a major theme when the story of our early-twenty-first-century national reset and renewal is written.

I noted earlier our paradoxical American character, how we are by nature both crazed, giddy grasshoppers and reliable, hardworking ants. Embracing our amateur spirit is an extension of that same paradox. It leads us to indulge our native chutzpah—*live the dream! to hell with the naysayers!*—but as a practical matter it also requires a profound humility, since the amateur must throw himself into situations where he's uncertain and even ignorant, and therefore obliged to figure out new ways of seeing problems and fresh ways of solving them. At this particular inflection point, after the crash and before the rebuild, frankly admitting that we aren't absolutely certain how to proceed is liberating, and crucial.

I like paradoxes, which is why, even though I'm not particularly religious, Zen Buddhism has always appealed to me. Take the paradoxical state that Buddhists seek to achieve, what they call *sho-shin*, or "beginner's mind." The twentieth-century Japanese Zen master Shunryu Suzuki, who spent the last dozen years of his life in America, wrote that "in the beginner's mind there are many possibilities, but in the expert's mind there are few." Which sounds to me very much like the core of Daniel Boorstin's amateur spirit. "The main obstacle to progress is not ignorance," Boorstin wrote, "but the illusion of knowledge."

And this isn't just a matter of airy-fairy philosophy: it's real, and it works. Not long before the movie director Danny Boyle won his Academy Award for *Slumdog Millionaire*, he was talking about the intense pleasure of making his first films, a dozen years earlier, when he literally had a beginner's mind. "There's something about that innocence and joy," he said, "when you don't quite know what you're doing." A decade after Steve Jobs founded Apple Computer, he was purged by his own board, but when the sense of betrayal passed, and he went on to create Pixar and oversee Apple's glorious renewal, he realized his personal reset had been a blessing in disguise. "The heaviness of being successful," Jobs has said of his firing, "was replaced by the lightness of being a beginner again, less sure about everything. It freed me to enter one of the most creative periods of my life." I happen to know what Jobs means: my sacking as editor of *New York* magazine thirteen years ago freed me to reinvent myself as a novelist and public radio host. Getting fired was traumatic. Finding my way since has been thrilling and immensely gratifying.

Thinking the Unthinkable

Although the famous Chinese curse "May you live in interesting times" is not, in fact, a Chinese curse, given China's enabling role in our present predicament, it ought to be. Since 2007, almost 40 percent of the value of publicly traded companies has evaporated, along with several trillion dollars' worth of home equity—at least $10,000 per American man, woman, and child—and five million jobs. Iconic businesses and whole industries are variously dead and dying.

But these times are not just accursed, not simply an awful episode to be endured—they really are *interesting* times, because of the new and possibly improved America that might be created out of the wreckage. Last fall, the unthinkable became thinkable and then, in the matter of a few weeks, actual. A signature phrase of the decade, "shock and awe," suddenly had an additional, domestic meaning.

As the recession ends and the sense of crisis fades, we mustn't lose our freshly, painfully acquired ability to think the unthinkable. We need to keep downside risks in mind, to remember that good times can dramatically end and systems suddenly fail. But as we plot our national reconstruction and reinvention, it's just as important—and maybe more so—to imagine the unimaginable on the *upside*. As we gasp in horror at our half glass of water, we really can—must—see it as half-full as well as half-empty.

This reset moment will not last for long, let alone forever. History and the zeitgeist keep moving. It's a good bet that the 2020s will be fully roaring, the dawn of yet another thrilling, crazy era of hyper-capitalist easy money and overnight fortunes and conspicuous consumption. As I've explained, the American character seems incurably bipolar.

So this next couple of years is our window of opportunity for a carefully considered reset. The elements of the untenable status quo, most obviously and critically how we use energy and pay for health care and educate our citizens, but also the ways we define contentment, are not immutable givens. Rather, they are the results of choices we made and habits we acquired and systems we built back in the twentieth century. Different, twenty-first-century choices are now available to us. Dysfunction and profligacy aren't inevitable, and the American tendency to magical thinking can be kept in check. The die-hard opposition of powerful institutions (oil companies, agribusiness, the health care industry, teachers' unions, and more) to fundamental change is implacable, for sure, but it isn't invincible. We can rediscover common sense and the better angels of our nature. We possess the ability to rejigger and renovate our lives and our country as necessary. But to get there, we have to keep thinking the unthinkable.

Acknowledgments

I am deeply grateful once again to my surpassingly smart and nimble Random House colleagues, especially Gina Centrello, Jennifer Hershey, Tom Perry, Sally Marvin, and Courtney Moran. At William Morris, Suzanne Gluck and Erin Malone continue to make my professional life easier than I have any right to expect. At *Time*—in addition to the indispensable Rick Stengel, who started this ball rolling— Romesh Ratnesar provided valuable nudges and John Huey's enthusiasm was amazing. Henry Finder and Jared Hohlt helped shape ideas that previously appeared in *The New Yorker* and *New York*, respectively. Without the help of my terrific *Studio 360* colleagues—you know who you are—I wouldn't have had the illuminating conversations with the people whose inspiring career changes I describe. And warmest, profoundest thanks to Anne Kreamer, as always, for being my first reader and closest pal.

About the Author

KURT ANDERSEN is the author of the novels *Heyday* and *Turn of the Century.* He is also the host and co-creator of the Peabody Award–winning public radio program *Studio 360* and a contributor to *Vanity Fair.* He was a co-founder of *Spy* magazine and the editor in chief of *New York,* and he has been a columnist, critic, and essayist for *The New Yorker, New York,* and *Time.* Andersen lives with his wife and daughters in Brooklyn.

About the Type

This book was set in Photina, a typeface designed by José Mendoza in 1971. It is a very elegant design with high legibility, and its close character fit has made it a popular choice for use in quality magazines and art gallery publications.